Long Time, No See

A man left for work one Friday afternoon, Instead of going home, he spent the entire weekend hunting and fishing with the boys and spending all of his wages. When he finally got home on Sunday night, he was confronted by his very angry wife. After two hours, she stopped nagging and asked, "How would you like it if you didn't see me for two or three days?" He replied, "That would be fine with me." Monday went by and he didn't see his wife, Tuesday and Wednesday came and went with the same results. Thursday, the swelling went down just enough to for him to see her just a little out of the corner of his left eye.

How About a Little Privacy?

Joan, who was rather well-proportioned, spent almost all of her vacation sunbathing on the roof of her hotel. She wore a bathing suit the first day, but on the second, she decided that no one could see her way up there, and she slipped out of it for an overall tan. She'd hardly begun when she heard someone running up the stairs. She was lying on her stomach, so she just pulled a towel over her rear. "Excuse me, miss," said the flustered assistant manager of the hotel, out of breath from running up the stairs. "The Hilton doesn't mind your sunbathing on the roof, but we would very much appreciate your wearing a bathing suit as you did yesterday." "What difference does it make?" Joan asked rather calmly. "No one can see me up here, and besides, I'm covered with a towel." "Not exactly," said the embarrassed man. "You're lying on the dining room skylight."

With Respects

As a bagpiper, I play many gigs. Recently I was asked by a funeral director to play at a graveside service for a homeless man. He had no family or friends, so the service was to be at a pauper's cemetery in the Nova Scotia back country.

As I was not familiar with the backwoods, I got lost. I didn't stop for directions. I finally arrived an hour late and saw the funeral guy had evidently gone and the hearse was nowhere in sight. There were only the diggers and crew left and they were eating lunch. I felt badly and apologized to the men for being late.

I went to the side of the grave and looked down and the vault lid was already in place. I didn't know what else to do, so I started to play.

The workers put down their lunches and began to gather around. I played out my heart and soul for this man with no family and friends. I played like I've never played before for this homeless man.

And as I played "Amazing Grace", the workers began to weep. They wept, I wept, we all wept together.

When I finished, I packed up my bagpipes and started for my car. Though my head was hung low, my heart was full.

As I opened the door to my car, I heard one of the workers say, "I never seen anything like that before, and I've been putting in septic tanks for twenty years."

Heaven Knows

A man dies and goes to Heaven. He gets to meet GOD and asks GOD if he can ask him a few questions. "Sure," GOD says, "Go right ahead". "OK," the man says. "Why did you make women so pretty?" GOD says, "So you would like them." "OK," the guy says. "But how come you made them so beautiful?" "So you would LOVE them", GOD replies. The man ponders a moment and then asks, "But why did you make them such airheads?" GOD says, "So they would love you!"

What To Do?

An American tourist is visiting China. After visiting all the tourist attractions he decides to inquire about the people and asks his guide: "How large is the population here?" "Around 1.5 billion" -- the guide answers. American, After a short pause: "So, what else do you do here?"

Circus Life

A husband and wife who work for the circus go to an adoption agency. Social workers there raise doubts about the living conditions in a circus, but the couple produce photos of their 50-foot luxury motor home, which is clean and well-maintained and equiped with a beautiful nursery.

The Social workers also raised concerns about the education of a child would receive while in the couple's care. "We've arranged for a full-time tutor who will teach the child all the usual subjects along with French, Mandarin and computer skills."

The Social workers are finally satisfied and ask, "What age child are you hoping to adopt?"

"It doesn't matter as long as the kid fits in the cannon."

NYC Tourist

A tourist is visiting New York City when his car breaks down. He jumps out and starts fiddling under the hood. About five minutes later, he hears some thumping sounds and looks around to see someone taking stuff out of his trunk! He runs around and yells, "Hey, bud, this is my car!" "OK," the man says, "You take the front and I'll take the back."

Everything is Bigger in Texas

There was a little old lady from a small town in America who had to go to Texas. She was amazed at the size of her hotel and her suite. She went into the huge cafe and said to the waitress, who took her order for a cup of coffee, that she had never before seen anything as big as the hotel or her suite. "Everything's big in Texas ma'am," said the waitress. The coffee came in the biggest cup the old lady had ever seen. "I told you, ma'am, that everything is big in Texas," said the waitress. On her way back to her suite, the old lady got lost in the vast corridors. She opened the door of a darkened room and fell into an enormous swimming pool. "Please!" she screamed. "Don't flush it!"

Friendship Pledge

Keep a SMILE on your face ~ And a SONG in your heart!

A smile - is a sign of joy.

A hug - is a sign of love.

A laugh - is a sign of happiness.

And a friend like me? - Well that's just a sign of good taste!

We'll be friends until I'm senile.

Then we'll be NEW friends!

Beautiful Wife

The 75 year old man and his young, knockout wife were shopping in an upscale jewelry boutique when the man's oldest friend bumped into him. Eyeing the curvaceous blonde bending over the counter to try on a necklace, the friend asked "How in the hell did YOU land a wife like that?" The old man whispered back, "Easy. I told her I was 90!"

Grandma

On a flight to Florida, I was preparing my notes for one of the parent-education seminars I conduct as an educational psychologist. The elderly woman sitting next to me explained that she was returning to Miami after having spent two weeks visiting her six children, 18 grandchildren and ten great-grandchildren in Boston. Then she inquired what I did for a living. I told her, fully expecting her to question me for free professional advice. Instead she sat back, picked up a magazine and said, "If there's anything you want to know, just ask me."

$100

Having dinner over at his friends house, Mike accidentally drops his napkin on the floor.

When he bends down under the table to pick it up, he notices that Bill's wife is not wearing any underwear.

Later, Mike goes into the kitchen to get some refreshments. Bill's wife follows him and asks, "Did you see anything that you liked under there?"

Mike admits that he did. She says, "You can have it, but it will cost you $100."

They decide that Mike should come to her house around 2 pm. on Friday while Bill is at work.

On Friday, Mike arrives at 2 pm. He pays Bill's wife $100. They go to the bedroom, have sex and then John leaves.

When Bill comes home at 6 pm, he asks his wife, "Did Mike come by this afternoon?"

Reluctantly, she replies, "Yes, he did stop by for a few minutes."

Next Bill asks, "Did he give you $100?"

"Oh hell, he knows!" she thinks to herself. Finally, she admits, "Well, yes, he did give me $100."

"Good," Bill says. "Mike came by the office this morning and borrowed $100 from me. He said that he would stop by our house on his way home and pay me back."

Shhhhh

An elderly man was having hearing problems and went to see a specialist. The doctor fitted him with hearing aids that brought his hearing back to full strength.

After a few weeks the man came back to make sure the new equipment was working properly, which it was.

The hearing specialist said: "It all seems perfect. Your family should be delighted you can hear everything now."

"Oh no," said the man, "I haven't told any of them. I just sit quietly, listening carefully. I've changed my will four times."

Advantage of Aging

* Your supply of brain cells is finally down to a manageable size.

* You are no longer viewed as a hypochondriac.

* People call you at 9:00 Am and ask "Did I wake you?"

* Your joints are more accurate at predicting the weather than the guy on TV.

* You can finally quit trying to hold in your stomach no matter who walks into the room.

Black Magic

An old man and woman were married for years and years even though they hated each other. When they had an argument, screams and yelling could be heard deep into the night. Repeatedly a threat was heard from the old man against his wife. "When I die I will dig my way out of the grave to come back and haunt you for the rest of your life!"

It was believed that the old man practiced black magic and was responsible for missing cats and dogs and strange sounds at all hours. He was feared and he enjoyed the respect it garnished.

The old man died abruptly under strange circumstances and the funeral had a closed casket. After the burial, the wife went straight to the local bar and began to party as if there was no tomorrow. Her actions were becoming extreme when her neighbors approached to ask a question: "Are you not afraid? Concerned? Worried? that this man who practiced black magic would dig his way up and out to come back to haunt you for the rest of your life?"

The wife put down her drink and said, "Let the old guy dig. I had him buried upside down!"

Remembering

A man walks into a bar and has a couple of beers. Once he is done the bartender tells him he owes $9.00. "But I paid, don't you remember?" says the customer. "Okay," says the bartender, "If you said you paid, you did." The man then goes outside and tells the first person he sees that the bartender can't keep track of whether his customers have paid. The second man then rushes in, orders a beer and later pulls the same stunt. The barkeep replies, "If you say you paid, I'll take your word for it." Soon the customer goes into the street, sees an old friend, and tells him how to get free drinks. The man hurries into the bar and begins to drink high-balls when, suddenly, the bartender leans over sand says, "You know, a funny thing happened in here tonight. Two men were drinking beer, neither paid and both claimed that they did. The next guy who tries that is going to get punched right in the nose." "I can't be bothered with your problems," the final patron responds. "Just give me my change and I'll be on my way."

Love, Mom

Sam invited his mother over for diner. During the course of the meal, Sam's mother couldn't help but notice how beautiful Sam's roommate Jennifer was. Mike's mom had long been suspicious of the "platonic" relationship between Jennifer and Sam, and this had only made her more curious.

Over the course of the evening, while watching the two interact, she started to wonder if there was more between Sam and Jennifer than met the eye.

Reading his mom's thoughts, Sam volunteered, "I know what you must be thinking, but I assure you Jennifer and I are just roommates."

About a week later, Jennifer came to Sam saying, "Ever since your mom came to dinner, I've been unable to find that beautiful silver gravy ladle. You don't suppose she took it, do you?" Sam said, "Well, I doubt it, but I 'll send her an e-mail just to be sure."

So Sam sat down and sent her a message.

"Dear Mom,

I'm not saying that you did take the gravy ladle from the house, I'm not saying that you did not take the gravy ladle. But the fact remains that it has been missing ever since you were here for diner.

Love, Sam"

Next Page ⟶

Love, Mom ....continued

Several days later, Sam received an email back from his mother that read"

"Dear Son,

I'm not saying that you do sleep with Jennifer, I'm not saying that you do not sleep with Jennifer. But the fact remains that if Jennifer was sleeping in her own bed, she would have found the gravy ladle by now.

Love, Mom"

Dead Penguins

Did you ever wonder why there are no dead penguins on the ice in Antarctica? Where do they go?

It is a know fact that penguins are a ritualistic bird that lives an extremely ordered life. Penguins are very committed to family and will mate for life.

If a penguin is found dead, other members of the family and social circle have been known to dig a hole in the ice, using their vestigial wings and beaks, until the hole is deep enough for the dead bird to be rolled into, and buried.

The male penguins then gather in a circle above the fresh grave and sing.

"Freeze a jolly good fellow."

"Freeze a jolly good fellow."

Where Are We

An American man, a Russian man, and an African man were all up in a hot-air balloon together. After a few minutes, the Russian man put his hand down through the clouds. "Aaah!" he said. "We're right over my homeland." "How can you tell?" asked the American. "I can feel the cold air." he replied. A few hours later the African man put his hand through the clouds. "Aah we're right over my homeland." he said. "How do you know that?" asked the Russian. "I can feel the heat of the desert." Several more hours later the American put his hand through the clouds. "Aah, we're right over New York City." The Russian and the African were amazed. "How do you know all of that?" they exclaimed. The American pulled his hand up. "My watch is missing."

Work Week

A father is asked by his friend, "Has your son decided what he wants to be when he grows up?" "Yes, he wants to be a garbage collector," he replies to this his friend responds, "Strange ambition to have for a career." "Well, he thinks that garbage collectors only work on Tuesdays and Thursdays!"

Elderly Exercise

I'm at the emergency room. Today was not a good day. I decided to go horseback riding, something I haven't done in many years.

It turned out to be a big mistake! I got on the horse and started out slow, but then we went a little faster and before I knew it, we were going as fast as the horse could go. I couldn't take the pace and fell off, but caught my foot in the stirrup with the horse dragging me.

It wouldn't stop!

Thank goodness the manager at Toys-R-Us came out and unplugged the machine.

3 Golfers

A priest, a doctor, and an engineer were waiting one morning for a particularly slow group of golfers.

The engineer fumed, "What's with those guys? We must have been waiting for fifteen minutes!"

The doctor chimed in, "I don't know, but I've never seen such inept golf!"

The priest said, "Here comes the greens-keeper. Let's have a word with him." He said, "Hello George, What's wrong with that group ahead of us? They're rather slow, aren't they?"

The greens-keeper replied, "Oh, yes. That's a group of blind firemen. They lost their sight saving our clubhouse from a fire last year, so we always let them play for free anytime!"

The group fell silent for a moment. The priest said, "That's so sad. I think I will say a special prayer for them tonight."

The doctor said, "Good idea. I'm going to contact my ophthalmologist colleague and see if here's anything she can do for them."

The engineer said, "Why can't they play at night?"

Pregnancy and Exercise

The room was full of pregnant women with their husbands. The instructor said, "Ladies, remember that exercise is good for you. Walking is especially beneficial. It strengthens the pelvic muscles and will make delivery that much easier. Just pace yourself, make plenty of stops and try to stay on a soft surface like grass or a path. "Gentlemen, remember -- you're in this together. It wouldn't hurt you to go walking with her. In fact, that shared experience would be good for you both."

The room became very quiet as the men absorbed and pondered this information. After a few moments a man at the back of the room, slowly raised his hand. "Yes?" asked the instructor. "I was just wondering if it would be all right if she carried a golf bag?"

Modern Relationships

One woman to another at a singles bar: "I'm not as optimistic about relationships as I used to be. These days, when I meet a man, I ask myself, "Is this the guy I want my children to spend every other weekend with?"

Bear Warning Sign

The Forest Service has issued a Bear Warning in the National Forests for the summer. They're urging people to protect themselves by wearing bells and carrying pepper spray.

Campers should be alert for signs of fresh bear activity, and they should be able to tell the difference between Black Bear and Grizzly Bear dung. Black Bear dung is rather small and round.

Sometimes you can see fruit seeds and or squirrel fur in it.

Grizzly Bear dung has bells in it and smells like pepper spray!

Afternoon Delight

Bill and Martha decided that the only way to pull off a Sunday afternoon quickie with their 10 year old son in the apartment was to send him out on the balcony and order him to report on all the neighborhood activities.

The boy began his commentary as his parents put their plan into motion.

"There's a car being towed from the parking lot," he said.

"An ambulance just drove by."

A few moments passed.

"Looks like the Andersons' have company." he called out.

"Matt's riding a new bike and the Coopers are having sex."

Mom and Dad shot up in bed. "How do you know that?" the startled father asked.

"Their kid is standing out on the balcony too," his son replied.

Old Blue

A man was opening a wildlife park and was needing a bear for an exhibit. He called some hunters and asked them if they could recommend someone who specialized in taking big game alive. They told him about a man that was a little unorthodox but the best in the business. He called the specialist and made arrangements to meet him at a spot in the woods where a bear had recently been spotted. After waiting a while an old beat up pickup backed in next to him. An old man jumped out and started unloading an unusual assortment of items. He took out a feather, some rope, a gun, and an old hunting dog. 'What are you going to do with all of this? Asked the park owner. "Well this is Old Blue," the old man said referring to the dog, "He's the best tracking dog there ever was. He is going to track the bear down and run him up a tree.

Next Page

Old Blue ...continued

I'm going to climb the tree with this feather and start tickling the bear. That will loosen his grip and he will fall out of the tree. Old Blue is trained to lunge between his legs as soon as he hits the ground and bite down with all of his might. The bear will throw his arms up in pain. That's when you take the rope and tie him up and we've got him." The old man said. "Wait a minute" Said the park owner. I want to take the bear alive. What's the gun for?" The old man looks at the gun and says "That's in case the bear knocks me out of the tree first.........then you shoot Old Blue!"

Pet Names

An elderly gent was invited to his friends' home for dinner one evening. He was impressed by the way his buddy preceded every request to his wife with endearing terms - Honey, My Love, Darling, Pumpkin, etc.

The couple had been married almost 70 years, and clearly they were still very much in love. While the wife was in the kitchen, the man leaned over and said to his host, "I think it's wonderful that, after all these years, you still call your wife those loving pet names."

The old man hung his head. "I have to tell you the truth," he said, "I forgot her name about 10 years ago."

Old New Friend

Grandpa was telling his young grandson what life was like when he was a boy. "In the winter we'd ice skate on our pond. In the summer we could swim in the pond, and pick berries in the woods. We'd swing on an old tire my dad hung from a tree on a rope. And we had a pony we rode all over the farm"

The little boy was amazed, and sat silently for a minute. Finally he said, "Grandpa, I wish I'd gotten to know you a lot sooner!"

Seeing the Light

An older couple go to the doctor. The old man goes first to have his physical. He finishes and it is the wife's turn. The Dr. says."Before we start, I'd like to talk to you about your husband.

"I asked your husband how he was feeling, he told me he was great. He said that when he got up to go to the bathroom last night God turned on the light for him and when he finished and shut the door God turned out the light for him. Does this make any sense to you?"

Dammit", the old woman responded, "He's peeing in the fridge again."

Short Term Memory Loss

A couple in their 90's are both having some short term memory loss. While in for a checkup, the doctor says that physically they are okay, but since they're having trouble remembering things they might want to start writing things down.

Later that evening they are sitting and reading, when the husband gets up. "Would you like anything from the kitchen?" he asks.

"Some vanilla ice cream," his wife replies.

"Okay"

"Should you write that down so you don't forget?" she asks.

"Don't worry, I won't forget."

"Well" she says. "A few raspberries on top would be great. You want to write that down?"

"I got it, honey. A bowl of vanilla ice cream with raspberries on top."

"And chocolate sauce, too. Maybe you'll forget that. Want me to write it down for you?"

He replies" I got it, I got it, I got it"

He waddles out to the kitchen. A half hour later he returns with a plate of ham and scrambled eggs and gives it to his wife.

She stares at the plate a few seconds, then says, "You forgot my toast!"

All In A Days Work

Two paddies were working for the city public works department. One would dig a hole and the other would follow behind him and fill the hole in. They worked up one side of the street, then down the other, then moved on to the next street, working furiously all day without rest, one man digging a hole, the other filling it in again. An onlooker was amazed at their hard work, but couldn't understand what they were doing. So he asked the hole digger, "I'm impressed by the effort you two are putting in to your work, but I don't get it - why do you dig a hole, only to have your partner follow behind and fill it up again?" The hole digger wiped his brow and sighed, "Well, I suppose it probably looks odd because we're normally a three-person team. But today the lad who plants the trees called in sick.'"

Mistaken Identity

A guy goes to the supermarket and notices an attractive woman waving at him. She says hello. He's rather taken aback because he can't place where he knows her from. So he says, "Do you know me?" To which she replies, "I think you're the father of one of my kids." Now his mind travels back to the only time he has ever been unfaithful to his wife and says, "My God, are you the stripper from my bachelor party that I made love to on the pool table?"
She looks into his eyes and says calmly, "No, I'm your son's teacher."

Golf Pro Advice

A young woman was taking golf lessons and had just started playing her first round of golf when she suffered a bee sting. Her pain was so intense that she decided to return to the clubhouse for medical assistance. The golf pro saw her heading back and said, "You are back early, what's wrong?" "I was stung by a bee!" she said. "Where?" he asked. "Between the first and second hole." she replied. He nodded and said, "Your stance is far too wide."

Jealousy

After a long night of making love, the guy notices a photo of another man, on the woman's nightstand by the bed. He begins to worry. "Is this your husband?" he nervously asks. "No, silly," she replies, snuggling up to him. "Your boyfriend, then?" he continues. "No, not at all," she says, nibbling away at his ear. "Is it your dad or your brother?" he inquires, hoping to be reassured. "No, no, no! You are so hot when you're jealous!" she answers. "Well, who in the hell is he, then?" he demands. She whispers in his ear: "That's me before the surgery."

Blind Man In A Biker Bar

A blind man wanders into an all Girls Biker Bar in London, England by mistake.

He finds his way to a bar stool and orders a drink. After sitting there for awhile, he yells to the barkeep, 'Hey, you wanna hear a blonde joke?'

The bar immediately falls absolutely silent. In a very deep, husky voice, the woman next to him says, 'Before you tell that joke, sir, I think it's only fair, given you are blind, to tell you you're in a girls biker bar and you should know five things:

1. The bartender is a blonde girl with a baseball bat.

2. The bouncer is a blonde girl.

3. I'm a 6-foot tall, 175 lb. blonde woman with a black belt in karate.

4. The woman sitting next to me is blonde and a professional weightlifter.

5. The lady to your right is blonde and a professional wrestler.

Now, think about it seriously 'Mister', do you still wanna tell that joke? "

The blind man thinks for a minute, sighs, shakes his head, and mutters, "No, it's a good joke, but not if I'm gonna have to explain it five times."

Services for a Passed Dog

Well, Patrick lived alone in the Irish countryside with only his pet dog for company. One day the dog died and Patrick went to the parish priest and asked Father, my dog died, could you say a mass for the poor creature? Father Michael replied, "I'm afraid not we can't have services for an animal in the church."
 But there are some Baptists down the lane who might do this. OK thanks Father, do you think $5,000.00 would be enough to donate to them for the service? Father exclaimed, "Sweet Mary and Joseph, why didn't you tell me the dog was Catholic! "

Bird Talk

A lady goes to her priest one day and tells him, "Father, I have a problem. I have two female parrots, but they only know how to say one thing."

"What do they say?" the priest inquired.

They say, "Hi, we're hookers! Do you want to have some fun?"

"That's obscene!" the priest exclaimed, Then he thought for a moment. "You know," he said, "I may have a solution to your problem. I have two male talking parrots, which I have taught to pray and read the Bible. Bring your two parrots over to my house, and we'll put them in the cage with Francis and Peter. My parrots can teach your parrots to praise and worship, and your parrots are sure to stop saying that phrase in no time."

Next Page

Bird Talk ...continued

"Thank you," the woman responded, "this may very well be the solution." The next day, she brought her female parrots to the priest's house. As he ushered her in, she saw that his two male parrots were inside their cage holding rosary beads and praying. Impressed, she walked over and placed her parrots in with them. After a few minutes, the female parrots cried out in unison: "Hi, we're hookers! Do you want to have some fun?"
There was stunned silence. Shocked, one male parrot looked over at the other male parrot and exclaimed, "Put the beads away, Frank. Our prayers have been answered!"

Younger Woman

A balding, white haired man walked into a jewelry store this past Friday evening with a beautiful much younger gal at his side. He told the jeweler he was looking for a special ring for his girlfriend.

The jeweler looked through his stock and brought out a $5,000 ring.

The man said, "No, I'd like to see something more special."

At that statement, the jeweler went to his special stock and brought another ring over.

"Here's a stunning ring at only $40,000", the jeweler said.

The lady's eyes sparkled and her whole body trembled with excitement.

Next Page

Younger Woman ...continued

The old man seeing this said, 'We'll take it.'

The jeweler asked how payment would be made and the man stated, "By check. I know you need to make sure my check is good, so I'll write it now and you can call the bank Monday to verify the funds; I'll pick the ring up Monday afternoon."

On Monday morning, the jeweler angrily phoned the old man and said "Sir...There's no money in that account."

"I know,' said the old man..."But let me tell you about my weekend."

Church Lady

An elderly woman had just returned to her home from an evening of church services when she was startled by an intruder. She caught the man in the act of robbing her home of its valuables and yelled, "Stop! Acts 2:38 (Repent and be baptized, in the name of Jesus Christ so that your sins may be forgiven.) The burglar stopped in his tracks. The woman calmly called the police and explained what she had done. As the officer cuffed the man to take him in, he asked the burglar, "Why did you just stand there? All the old lady did was yell a scripture to you." "Scripture?" replied the burglar. "She said she had an ax and two 38's!"

College Dog

A young cowboy from Montana goes off to college.

Halfway through the semester, having foolishly squandered all his money, he calls home. "Dad," he says, "You won't believe what modern education is developing! They actually have a program here in Missoula that will teach our dog, ol' Blue how to talk!"

"That's amazing," his Dad says, "How do I get ol' Blue in that program?"

"Just send him down here with $1,000," the young cowboy says, "and I'll get him in the course."

So his father sends the dog and the $1,000.

About two-thirds of the way through the semester, the money runs out again. The boy calls home.

"So how's ol' Blue doing son?" his father asks.

"Awesome, Dad, he's talking up a storm," the boy says, "but you just won't believe this -- they've had such good results they are now starting to teach the animals how to read!"

"Read!?" says his father, "No kidding! How do we get ol' Blue in that program?"

"Just send $2,500, I'll get him in the class."

Next Page

College Dog ...continued

The money promptly arrives. But our hero has a problem. At the end of the year, his father will find out the dog can neither talk, nor read.

So he shoots the dog.

When he arrives home at the end of the year, his father is all excited, "Where's ol' Blue? I just can't wait to see him read something and talk!"

"Dad," the boy says, "I have some grim news. Yesterday morning just before we left to drive home, ol' Blue was in the living room, kicked back in the recliner, reading the Wall Street Journal like he usually does."

"Then ol' Blue turned to me and asked, so, is your daddy still messing around with the little redhead who lives down the street?"

The father went white and exclaimed, "I hope you shot that son-of-a-bitch before he talks to your Mother!"

"I sure did, Dad!"

Cruise Ship Magician

A magician was working on a cruise ship in the Caribbean. The audience would be different each week, so the magician allowed himself to do the same tricks over and over again.

There was only one problem: The captain's parrot saw the shows every week and began to understand what the magician did in every trick. Once he understood that, he started shouting in the middle of the show.

"Look, it's not the same hat!" "Look, he's hiding the flowers under the table!" "Hey, why are all the cards the Ace of Spades?"

The magician was furious but couldn't do anything, it was the captain's parrot after all.

One day the ship had an accident and sank. The magician found himself on a piece of wood, in the middle of the ocean, and of course the parrot was by his side.

They stared at each other with hate, but did not utter a word. This went on for several days.

After a week the parrot finally said, "Okay, I give up. What did you do with the boat?"

Deep Thinking

Sherlock Holmes and Dr. Watson go on a camping trip. After a good dinner and a bottle of wine, they retire for the night, and go to sleep. Some hours later, Holmes wakes up and nudges his faithful friend. "Watson, look up at the sky and tell me what you see." "I see millions and millions of stars, Holmes" replies Watson. "And what do you deduce from that?" Watson ponders for a minute. "Well, Astronomically, it tells me that there are millions of galaxies and potentially billions of planets. Astrologically, I observe that Saturn is in Leo. I deduce that the time is approximately a quarter past three. Methodologically, I suspect that we will have a beautiful day tomorrow. Theologically, I can see that God is all powerful, and that we are a small and insignificant part of the universe." But what does it tell you, Holmes?" Holmes is silent for a moment. "Watson, you idiot!" he says. "Someone has stolen our tent!"

Material Possessions

The American doctor parked his brand new Lexus right in front of the hospital, ready to show it off to his colleagues. As he got out, an ambulance came along too close to the curb and completely tore off the driver's door.

Fortunately, a cop in a police car was close enough to see the accident and pulled up behind the Lexus, his lights flashing. But, before the cop had a chance to ask any questions, the doctor started screaming hysterically about how his Lexus, which he had just picked up the day before, was now completely ruined and would never be the same, no matter how the body shop tried to make it new again.

After the doctor finally wound down from his rant, the cop shook his head in disgust and disbelief. "I can't believe how materialistic you doctors are, " he said. "You are so focused on your possessions you neglect the most important things in life."

"How can you say such a thing?" asked the doctor.

The cop replied, "Don't you even realize your left arm is missing? It got ripped off when the ambulance hit you!!!"

"OH, MY GOD!" screamed the doctor....... "MY ROLEX IS GONE!"

Dogs

A little girl asked her Mom, "Mom, may I take the dog for a walk around the block?" Mom replies, "No, because she is in heat."

"What's that mean?" asked the child.

"Go ask your father", answered the mother, "I think he's in the garage." The little girl goes to the garage and says, "Dad, may I take Belle for a walk around the block? I asked Mom, but she said the dog was in heat, and to come to you."

Dad said, "Bring Belle over here"" He took a rag, soaked it with gasoline, and scrubbed the dog's backside with it and said, "Okay, you can go now, but keep Belle on the leash and only go one time around the block."

The little girl left, and returned a few minutes later with no dog on the leash. Surprised, Dad asked, "Where's Belle?"

"She ran out of gas about halfway down the block, so another dog is pushing her home."

Donkey Raffle

Young Chuck moved to Texas and bought a donkey from a farmer for $100.00.

The farmer agreed to deliver the donkey the next day. The next day the farmer drove up and said, "Sorry, son, but I have some bad news; the donkey died."

Chuck replied, 'Well, that's OK, just give me my money back." The farmer said, "Sorry, can't do that. I spent it already."

Chuck said, "'OK, then just bring me the dead donkey."

The farmer asked, "What are you going to do with him?" Chuck said, "I'm going to raffle him off." The farmer said, "You can't raffle off a dead donkey!" Chuck said, "Sure I can, watch me. I just won't tell anybody he's dead."

A month later, the farmer ran into Chuck. "What happened with the dead donkey?"

Chuck said, "I raffled him off. I sold 500 tickets at two dollars apiece and made a profit of $898.00."

The farmer asked, "Didn't anyone complain?"

Chuck said, "Just the guy who won. So I gave him his two dollars back."

DUI ...TEXAS Style

Recently a routine police patrol parked outside a bar in Austin, Texas. After last call the officer noticed a man leaving the bar so apparently intoxicated that he could barely walk.

The man stumbled around the parking lot for a few minutes, with the officer quietly observing. After what seemed an eternity in which he tried his keys on five different vehicles, the man managed to find his car and fall into it. He sat there for a few minutes as a number of other patrons left the bar and drove off.

Finally he started the car, switched the wipers on and off--it was a fine, dry summer night, flicked the blinkers on and off a couple of times, honked the horn and then switched on the lights.

He moved the vehicle forward a few inches, reversed a little and then remained still for a few more minutes as some more of the other patrons' vehicles left. At last, when his was the only car left in the parking lot, he pulled out and drove slowly down the road.

Next Page ⟩

DUI ..TEXAS Style ...continued

The police officer, having waited patiently all this time, now started up his patrol car, put on the flashing lights, promptly pulled the man over and administered a breathalyzer test. To his amazement, the breathalyzer indicated no evidence that the man had consumed any alcohol at all!

Dumbfounded, the officer said, I'll have to ask you to accompany me to the police station. This breathalyzer equipment must be broken.

"I doubt it", said the truly proud Redneck. 'Tonight I'm the designated decoy.'

Coffee

The local courtroom was packed as testimony began in the sentencing hearing of a woman convicted of murdering her husband of 20 years by poisoning his coffee.

The defense attorney knew he had his work cut out for him trying to make his client appear more sympathetic to the Judge, especially since she had been so "matter-of-fact" about the whole thing all during the trial.

"Mrs. Roth," he began, "was there any point that morning where you felt pity for your husband ?" "Well... yeah... I guess..." she replied.

"And when was that?" pressed the attorney.

"Well...," she replied, "when he asked for his third cup."

I Just Thought...

One night, an 87-year-old woman came home from Bingo to find her husband in bed with another woman. Angry, she became violent and ended up pushing him off the balcony of their apartment, killing him instantly. When brought before the court on charges of murder, she was asked if she had anything to say to defend herself. "Well, Your Honor," she replied coolly. "I figured that at 92, if he could make love to another woman, he could fly!"

First Fight

Three weeks after her wedding day, Joanna called her minister. "Reverend," she wailed, "John and I had a DREADFUL fight!"
"Calm down, my child," said the minister, "it's not half as bad as you think. Every marriage has to have its first fight!"
"I know, I know!" said Joanna. "But what am I going to do with the BODY?"

New York Gang in Heaven

One day at the entrance to heaven, St. Peter saw a New York street gang. walk up to the Pearly Gates. This being a first, St. Peter ran to God and said, "God, there are some evil, thieving New Yorkers at the Pearly Gates. What do I do?". God replied, "Just do what you normally do with that type. Re-direct them down to hell." St. Peter went back to carry out the order and all of a sudden he comes running back yelling "God, God, they're gone, they're gone!" "Who, the New Yorkers?". "No, the Pearly Gates."

Three Wishes

A man was walking on the beach one day and he found a bottle half buried in the sand. He decided to open it. Inside was a genie. The genie said," I will grant you three wishes and three wishes only." The man thought about his first wish and decided, "I think I want 1 million dollars transferred to a Swiss bank account. POOF! Next he wished for a Ferrari red in color. POOF! There was the car sitting in front of him. He asked for his final wish, " I wish I was irresistible to women." POOF! He turned into a box of chocolates.

Wisdom Of Age

Of course I talk to myself, sometimes I need expert advice!!!

I don't have gray hair. I have "wisdom highlights". I'm just very wise.

I don't need anger management. I need people to stop pissing me off!

My people skills are just fine. It's my tolerance to idiots that needs work.

Even duct tape can't fix stupid ... but it can muffle the sound!

I'm going to retire and live off of my savings. Not sure what I'll do that second week.

The kids text me "plz" which is shorter than please. I text back "no" which is shorter than "yes".

I don't trip over things, I do random gravity checks!

The biggest lie I tell myself is ..."I don't need to write that down, I'll remember it."

If God wanted me to touch my toes, he would've put them on my knees.

GI Insurance

Airman Jones was assigned to the induction center, where he advised new recruits about their government benefits, especially their GI insurance. It wasn't long before Captain Smith noticed that Airman Jones was having a staggeringly high success-rate, selling insurance to nearly 100% of the recruits he advised. Rather than ask about this, the Captain stood in the back of the room and listened to Jones' sales pitch. Jones explained the basics of the GI Insurance to the new recruits, and then said: "If you have GI Insurance and go into battle and are killed, the government has to pay $200,000 to your beneficiaries. If you don't have GI insurance, and you go into battle and get killed, the government only has to pay a maximum of $6000. Now," he concluded, "which group do you think they are going to send into battle first?"

Boundary Dispute

Did you know that heaven and hell are actually right next to each other? They are separated by a big chain-link fence. Well, one day hell was having a big party and it got a little out of hand. God heard the ruckus and arrived to find his fence completely smashed by the wild party goers. He called the devil over and said "Look, Satan, you have to rebuild this fence." Satan agreed. The next day God noticed that the devil had completely rebuilt the fence...but it was 2 feet further into heaven than before. "Satan!" beckoned God. "You have to take that fence down and put it back where it belongs!" "Yeah? What if I don't?" replied the devil. "I'll sue you if I have to," answered God. "Sure," laughed Satan. "Where are you going to find a lawyer?"

Childhood Wish

A man asked his wife, "What would you most like for your birthday?" She said, "I'd love to be ten again." On the morning of her birthday, he got her up bright and early and they went to a theme park. He put her on every ride in the park - the Death Slide, The Screaming Loop, the Wall of Fear. She had a go on every ride there was. She staggered out of the theme park five hours later, her head reeling and her stomach turning. Then off to a movie theater, popcorn, cola and sweets. At last she staggered home with her husband and collapsed into bed. Her husband leaned over and asked, "Well, dear, what was it like being ten again?" One eye opened and she groaned, "Actually, honey, I meant dress size!"

Got Viagra?

A woman is at home when she hears someone knocking at her door. She goes to the door opens it and sees a man standing there. He asks the lady, "Do you have a Vagina?" She slams the door in disgust. The next morning she hears a knock at the door, its the same man and he asks the same question to the woman, "Do you have a Vagina?" She slams the door again. Later that night when her husband gets home she tell him what has happened for the last two days. The husband tells his wife in a loving and concerned voice, "Honey, I am taking an off day tomorrow so as to be home, just in case this guy shows up again." The next morning they hear a knock at the door and both ran for the door. The husband whispers to the wife, "Honey, I'm going to hide behind the door and listen and if it is the same guy I want you to answer yes to the question because I want to a see where he's going with this." She nods yes to her husband and opens the door. Sure enough the same fellow is standing there, he asks, "Do you have a Vagina?" "Yes I do." says the lady. The man replies, "Good, would you mind telling your husband to leave my wife's alone and start using yours!"

Granny In The Hospital

A sweet grandmother telephoned St. Joseph 's Hospital. She timidly asked, "Is it possible to speak to someone who can tell me how a patient is doing?"

The operator said, "I'll be glad to help, dear. What's the name and room number?"

The grandmother in her weak, tremulous voice said "Noreen, Room 302"

The operator replied, "Let me place you on hold while I check with her nurse." After a few minutes, the operator returned to the phone and said, "Oh, I have good news. Her nurse just told me that Noreen is doing very well. Her blood pressure is fine; her blood work just came back as normal, and her physician, Dr. Cohen, has scheduled her to be discharged on Tuesday."

The grandmother said, "Thank you. That's wonderful!

I was so worried God bless you for the good news."

The operator replied, "You're more than welcome. Is Noreen your daughter?"

The grandmother said, "No, I'm Noreen in 302. No one tells me anything."

Secret of Aging

A woman walked up to a little old man rocking in a chair on his porch. "I couldn't help noticing how happy you look," she said. "What's your secret for a long happy life?" "I smoke three packs of cigarettes a day," he said. "I also drink a case of whiskey a week, eat fatty foods, and never exercise." "That's amazing," the woman said. "How old are you?' "Twenty-six," he said.

Golf Wisdom

One day, a grandpa and his grandson go golfing. The young one is really good and the old one is just giving him tips. They are on hole 8 and there is a tree in the way and the grandpa says, "When I was your age, I would hit the ball right over that tree." So, the grandson hits the ball and it bumps against the tree and lands not to far from where it started. "Of course," added the grandpa, "when I was your age, the tree was only 3 feet tall."

Homework Help

At dinner, Seth said to his father, "Dad, I got into trouble at school today and it's all your fault." "How's that?" asked the master of the house. "Remember I asked you how much $500,000 was?" "Yeah, I remember." "Well, 'a helluva lot' ain't the right answer."

Heavy Luggage

A businessman was having a tough time lugging his lumpy, oversized travel bag onto the plane. Helped by a flight attendant, he finally managed to stuff it in the overhead bin. "Do you always carry such heavy luggage?" she sighed. "No more," the man said. "Next time, I'm riding in the bag, and my partner can buy the ticket!"

Irish Miracle

An Irish priest is driving down to New York and gets stopped for speeding in Connecticut. The state trooper smells alcohol on the priest's breath and then sees an empty wine bottle on the floor of the car.

He says, "Sir, have you been drinking?"

"Just water," says the priest.

The trooper says, "Then why do I smell wine?"

The priest looks at the bottle and says, "Good Lord! He's done it again!"

Price of High Fashion

A lady walks into Harrods. She looks around, spots a beautiful diamond bracelet and walks over to inspect it. As she bends over to look more closely, she unexpectedly farts.

Very embarrassed, she looks around nervously to see if anyone noticed her little woops, and prays that a sales person was not anywhere near.

As she turns around her worst nightmare materializes in the form of a salesman standing right behind her - Good looking as well.

Cool as a cucumber, he displays all the qualities one would expect of a professional in a store like Harrods.

He politely greets the lady with " Good day Madam, How may we help you today?"

Blushing and uncomfortable, but still hoping that the salesman somehow missed her little "incident", she asks, "What is the price of this lovely bracelet?"

He answers, "Madam, - if you farted just looking at it- you're gonna shit yourself when I tell you the price!"

Pity of Getting Old

When I went to lunch today, I noticed an old man sitting on a park bench sobbing his eyes out. I stopped and asked him what was wrong. He said, "I have a 26 year old wife at home. She rubs my back every morning and then gets up and makes me pancakes, sausage, fresh fruit and freshly ground coffee."
I said, "Well, then why are you crying?"
He said, "She makes me homemade soup for lunch and my favorite brownies, cleans the house and then watches sports TV with me for the rest of the afternoon."
I said, "Well, why are you crying?"
He said, "For dinner she makes me a gourmet meal with wine and my favorite dessert and then makes love with me until the wee hours"
I said, "Well, why in the world would you be crying?"
He said, "I can't remember where I live!"

More Wisdom Of Age

* Wouldn't it be great if we could put ourselves in the dryer for ten minutes; come out wrinkle-free and three sizes smaller!

* Last year I joined a support group for procrastinators. We haven't met yet!

* Old age is coming at a really bad time!

* Lord grant me the strength to accept the things I cannot change, the courage to change the things I can and the friends to post my bail when I finally snap!

* Why do I have to press one for English when you're just gonna transfer me to someone I can't understand anyway?

* At my age "Getting lucky" means walking into a room and remembering what I came in there for.

State Police

Sitting on the side of the highway waiting to catch speeding drivers, a State Police Officer sees a car puttering along at 22 MPH. He thinks to himself, "This driver is just as dangerous as a speeder!" So he turns on his lights and pulls the driver over. Approaching the car, he notices that there are five old ladies -two in the front seat and three in the back -wide eyed and white as ghosts. The driver, obviously confused, says to him,

"Officer, I don't understand, I was doing exactly the speed limit! What seems to be the problem?" "Ma'am," the officer replies, "you weren't speeding, but you should know that driving slower than the speed limit can also be a danger to other drivers."

State Police ...continued

"Slower than the speed limit? No sir, I was doing the speed limit exactly ...Twenty- two miles an hour!" the old woman says a bit proudly.

The State Police officer, trying to contain a chuckle explains to her that "22" was the route number, not the speed limit. A bit embarrassed, the woman grinned and thanked the officer for pointing out her error. "But before I let you go, Ma'am, I have to ask... Is everyone in this car OK? These women seem awfully shaken and they haven't muttered a single peep this whole time," the officer asks with concern.

"Oh, they'll be all right in a minute officer. We just got off Route 119."

Flip - Flop

Husband and wife.....

BEFORE MARRIAGE:

Husband - Aaah! ...At last! I can hardly wait!

Wife - Do you want me to leave?

Husband - No! Don't even think about it.

Wife - Do you love me?

Husband - Of course! Always have and always will!

Wife - Have you ever cheated on me?

Husband - No! Why are you even asking?

Wife - Will you kiss me?

Husband - Every chance I get!

Wife - Will you hit me?

Husband - Hell no! Are you crazy?!

Wife - Can I trust you?

Husband - Yes.

Wife - Darling!

AFTER MARRIAGE: read from bottom to top.

Last Wishes

While driving down a steep and curvy logging road, a group of biologists loose control of their 4-wheel drive SUV and careen down the hill. The truck piles up at the bottom of the canyon, and everyone aboard perishes. Surprisingly, they all go to heaven. At an orientation they are asked, "When you are in your casket and your friends and family are mourning about your death, what would you like to hear them say about you?" The first guy, a well known botanist says, "I would like to hear them say that I was one of the greatest botanists of my time, and left an eternal contribution to the botanical world." The second guy, an ornithologist, says, "I would like to hear that I was a wonderful birder and made a huge difference in the recovery of our bird populations." The last guy, a scruffy mammalogist, replies, "I would like to hear them say... 'LOOK, HE'S MOVING!!!' "

Leave Work Early?

Three women who work in the same office notice that their female boss has started leaving work early every day.

One day they decide that after she leaves, they'll take off early too. After all, she never calls or comes back, so how is she to know?

The brunette is thrilled to get home early. She does a little gardening, watches a movie and then goes to bed early.

The redhead is elated to be able to get in a quick workout at the health club before meeting a dinner date.

The blonde is also very happy to be home early, but as she goes upstairs she hears noises coming from her bedroom. She quietly opens the door and is mortified to see her husband in bed with HER BOSS!

Ever so gently, she closes the door and creeps out of her house.

The next day, the brunette and redhead talk about leaving early again, but when they asked the blonde if she wanted to leave early too, she said, "NO WAY! I almost got caught yesterday."

Limp Duck

A woman brought a very limp duck to the veterinary surgeon. As she laid her pet on the table, the vet pulled out a stethoscope and listened to the birds chest.

After a moment or two, the vet shook his head and sadly said, "I'm sorry ma'am, but your duck, Cuddles, has passed away."

The distressed woman said, "Are you sure?"

"Yes I am sure. Your duck is dead," replied the vet.

How can you be so sure?" she protested. I mean, you haven't any tests on him or anything. He might just be in a coma or something."

The vet rolled his eyes, turned around and left the room. He returned a few minutes later with a black labrador retriever. As the duck's owner looked on in amazement, the dog stood on his hind legs, put his front paws on the examination table and sniffed the duck from top to bottom.

Next Page

Limp Duck ...continued

He then looked up at the vet with sad eyes and shook his head. The vet patted the dog on his head and took him out of the room.

A few minutes later he returned with a cat. The cat delicately sniffed the duck from head to toe, sat back on his haunches and shook his head. The vet looked at the woman and said, "I'm sorry but as I said, this duck is 100% certifiably dead."

The vet turned to his computer terminal, hit a few keystrokes and produced a bill, which he handed to the woman.

The ducks owner still in shock took the bill. "$550 just to tell me my duck was dead?!?

The vet shrugged, "I'm sorry. If you had just taken my word for it, the bill would have been $50, but with the Lab Report and the Cat Scan, it's now $550."

Dinner Prayer

At dinner, a little boy was ordered to lead in prayer...

BOY: But I don't know how to pray.

DAD: Just pray for your family members, friends and neighbors, the poor, etc.

BOY: "Dear Lord" he started. Thank you for our visitors and their children, who finished all my cookies and ice cream. Bless them so they won't come again. Forgive our neighbor's son, who removed my sister's clothes and wrestled with her on her bed.

This coming Christmas, please send clothes to all those poor naked ladies on my daddy's iPhone and provide shelter for the homeless men who use mom's room when daddy is at work.

°°°AMEN°°°°

Dinner was canceled,

Loose Teeth

A dinner speaker was in such a hurry to get to his engagement that when he arrived and sat down at the head table, he suddenly realized that he had forgotten his false teeth. Turning to the man next to him he said, "I forgot my teeth." The man said, "No problem." He reached into his pocket and pulled out a pair of false teeth. "Try these," he said. The speaker tried them. "Too loose," he said. The man then said, "I have another pair - try these." The speaker tried them and responded, "Too tight." The man was not taken back at all. He then said, "I have one more pair. Try them." The speaker said, "They fit perfectly."With that he ate his meal and gave his speech. After the dinner meeting was over, the speaker went over to thank the man who had helped him. "I want to thank you for coming to my aid. Where is your office? I've been looking for a good dentist." The man replied, "I'm not a dentist. I'm an undertaker."

Loyalty

It was a dark, stormy, night. The Marine was on his first assignment, and it was guard duty. A General stepped out taking his dog for a walk. The nervous young Private snapped to attention, made a perfect salute, and snapped out, "Sir, Good Evening, Sir!" The General, out for some relaxation, returned the salute and said "Good evening soldier, nice night, isn't it?" Well it wasn't a nice night, but the Private wasn't going to disagree with the General, so the he saluted again and replied, "Sir, Yes Sir!" The General continued, "You know there's something about a stormy night that I find soothing, it's really relaxing. Don't you agree?" The Private didn't agree, but then the private was just a private, and responded, "Sir, Yes Sir!" The General, pointing at the dog, "This is a Golden Retriever, the best type of dog to train." The Private glanced at the dog, saluted yet again, and said, "Sir, Yes Sir!" The General continued "I got this dog for my wife." The Private simply said, "Good trade, Sir!"

One Armed Man

A man lost an arm when his golf cart rolled over on him on a down slope. He became very depressed because he loved to play golf. One day in his despair, he decided to commit suicide and end it all.

He got on an elevator and went to the top of a building to jump off.

He was standing on the ledge looking down and saw this man down on the sidewalk skipping along, whooping and kicking up his heels. He looked closer and saw that this man didn't have any arms at all.

He started thinking, "What am I doing up here feeling sorry for myself? I still have one good arm to do things with."

He thought, "There goes a man with no arms skipping down the sidewalk so happy, and going on with his life."

Next Page

One Armed Man ...continued

He hurried down to the sidewalk and caught up with the man with no arms. He told him how glad he was to see him because he lost one of his arms and felt useless and was going to kill himself.

He thanked him for saving his life and said he knew he could make it with one arm if the guy could go on with no arms.

The man with no arms began dancing and whooping and kicking up his heels again.

He asked, "Why are you so happy anyway?"

He said, "I'm NOT happy. My gentiles itch."

Heart-warming stories like this just bring a tear to my eyes..

Horse Sense

An out-of-town-er drove his car into a ditch in a desolated area.

Luckily, a local farmer came to help with his big strong horse named Buddy.

He hitched Buddy up to the car and yelled, "Pull, Nellie, pull!" Buddy didn't move.

Then the farmer hollered, "Pull, Buster, pull!" Buddy didn't respond.

Once more the farmer commanded, "Pull, Coco, pull!" Nothing.

Then the farmer nonchalantly said, "Pull, Buddy, pull!" And the horse easily dragged the car out of the ditch.

The motorist was most appreciative and very curious.

He asked the farmer why he called his horse by the wrong name three times.

"Well...

Buddy is blind and if he thought he was the only one pulling, he wouldn't even try!"

The Nun and the Blind Man

A nun in the convent walked into the bathroom where mother superior was taking a shower.

"There is a blind man to see you," she says. "Well, if he is a blind man, then it does not matter if I'm in the shower.

Send him in." The blind man walks into the bathroom, and mother superior starts to tell him how much she appreciates him working at the convent for them.

She goes on and on and 10 minutes later the man interrupts: "That's nice and all, ma'am, but you can put your clothes on now.

Where do you want me to put these blinds?

Three Men in a Boat

Three guys were fishing on a lake one day, when an angel appeared in the boat.

When the three astonished men had settled down enough to speak, the first guy asked the angel humbly, "I've suffered from back pain ever since I took shrapnel in the Vietnam War. Could you help me?" "Of course," the angel said, and when he touched the man's back, the man felt relief for the first time in years.

The second guy who wore very thick glasses and had a hard time reading and driving.

He asked if the angel could do anything about his poor eyesight.

The angel smiled, removed the man's glasses and tossed them into the lake.

When they hit the water, the man's eyes cleared and he could see everything distinctly.

When the angel turned to the third guy, the guy put his hands out defensively -- "Don't touch me!" he cried, "I'm on a disability pension."

Illegal Catch

There was a salmon fisherman who was out in the ocean fishing when his boat sank.

He was lucky enough to make to a deserted island where he had to survive on what he could find.

When the Coastguard eventually found him, the leader noticed there was a fire pit with California Condor feathers all around.

He went over to the fisherman and said, "You know, it's illegal to kill a California Condor, I'm afraid I'm going to have to arrest you." The fisherman protested for some time saying that he killed it because he was going to starve but eventually he calmed down.

"Out of curiosity" the coastguard asked, "What did it taste like?" The fisherman replied, " Well, it was kind of a mix between a snowy owl and a bald eagle."

Fishing From The Bridge

Two Irishmen were walking down the street with two salmon each under their arms. Two other Irishmen walking in the opposite direction see the two lucky fishermen and ask " How did you catch those ?" "Well its like this! Michael here holds my legs over the bridge, and I grab the salmon as they swim up the river. We got four salmon. A great days fishing!"

So the fish-less pair look at each other and agree to give it a try.

They get to the bridge and Sean calls to his friend, "Hold my legs now Paddy".

Well he is hanging there upside down for thirty minutes when he suddenly cries..

"pull me up, pull me up!!" Paddy asks " do you have a fish Sean?"............

No replies Sean, "there's a bloody train coming!!!!!!!!"

Late Night Drink

One night, after closing time a barman is sitting at his bar minding his own business, when a spectral hound floats in through the door.

The barman, being an exceptionally cool kind of guy, asks "yeah, what do you want?".

The phantom hound explains, in a haunting voice "I've lost my tail...... and cannot rest until a kindly barman stitches it back-on".

At this request the barman stands back astonished and says to the phantom dog.....

"Sorry, but we don't re-tail spirits at this time of night".

Indecent Employment

A cleaning woman was applying for a new position.

When asked why she left her last employment, she replied, "Yes, sir, they paid good wages, but it was the most ridiculously undignified place I ever worked.

They played a game called Bridge, and last night a lot of folks were there.

As I was about to bring in the refreshments, I heard a man say, "Lay down and let's see what you've got."Another man said, "I've got strength but no length." Another man says to the lady, "Take your hand off my trick!" I pretty near dropped dead just then, when the lady answered, "You jumped me twice when you didn't have the strength for one raise." Another lady was talking about protecting her honor and two other ladies were talking and one said, "Now it's time for me to play with your husband and you can play with mine." Well, I just got my hat and coat and as I was leaving, I hope to die if one of them didn't say, "Well, I guess we'll go home now.

This is the last rubber."

3 Important People

Yeltsin, Trump and Bill Gates were invited to have dinner with God.

During dinner he told them: I need three important people to send my message out to all the people: "Tomorrow I will destroy the earth." Yeltsin immediately called together his cabinet and told them: "I have two really bad news items for you: 1) God really exists and 2) Tomorrow He will destroy the earth." Trump called an emergency meeting of the Senate and Congress and told them: "I have good news and bad news: 1) The GOOD news is that God really does exist 2) The BAD news is, tomorrow He is going to destroy the earth." Bill Gates went back to Microsoft and very happily announced: "I have two fantastic announcements: 1) I am one of the three most important people on earth 2) The Year Y2K problem is solved."

Three Engineers

There are three engineers in a car; an electrical engineer, a chemical engineer and a Microsoft engineer.

Suddenly the car just stops by the side of the road, and the three engineers look at each other wondering what could be wrong.

The electrical engineer suggests stripping down the electronics of the car and trying to trace where a fault might have occurred.

The chemical engineer, not knowing much about cars, suggests that maybe the fuel is becoming emulsified and getting blocked somewhere.

Then, the Microsoft engineer, not knowing much about anything, comes up with a suggestion, 'Why don't we close all the windows, get out, get back in, open the windows again, and maybe it'll work !?'

Kids!

A little boy came downstairs crying late one night.

" What's wrong?" asked his mother.

"Do people really come from dust, like they said in church?" he sobbed.

"In a way they do," said his mother.

" And when they die do the turn back to dust?"

"Yes, they do.' The little boy began to cry again. "Well, under my bed there's someone either coming or going!"

A Child's Prayer

A mother was teaching her 3-year-old the Lord's prayer.
For several evenings at bedtime she repeated it after her mother.
One night she said she was ready to solo.
The mother listened with pride as she carefully enunciated each word, right up to the end of the prayer.
"Lead us not into temptation," she prayed, "but deliver us some E-mail, Amen."

Heart Transplant

The doctor comes to see his heart transplant patient.
"This is good news.
It is very unusual, but we have two donors to choose from for your new heart." The patient is pleased.
He asks, "What were their jobs?" "One was a teacher and the other was an accountant." "I'll take the accountant's heart," says the patient.
"I want one that hasn't been used."

Christmas Shopping

It was Christmas and the judge was in a merry mood as he asked the prisoner, "What are you charged with?" "Doing my Christmas shopping early," replied the defendant.
"That's no offense," said the judge. "How early were you doing this shopping?"
"Before the store opened," countered the prisoner.

Prison Humor

It was Rocky's first night in the penitentiary.

All of the inmates were in their cells and he was trying to become a bit more comfortable with his meager surroundings.

As he leaned against the bars at the front of his cell, Rocky heard a voice call out "44" and the whole cell block erupted into laughter! Another voice called "16" and again there was laughter.

A third voice called "62" which was followed by laughter throughout the block.

Rocky didn't know what was going on so he rapped on his cell wall. "Yeah, whaddaya want?" came the gruff reply from next door.

"What's going on, here?" asked Rocky.

Next Page

Prison Humor ...continued

"Well," said the other inmate, "down in the prison library there's only one joke book. We've all read the book so many times that we don't waste time telling the joke, we just call out it's number." So the next day Rocky went down to the library and, sure enough, found r the yellowed, dog-eared joke book and read it from cover to cover.

That night, wanting to be part of the group, Rocky confidently called out "44" and everyone laughed!

He tried calling "16" and "62" and again there were peals of laughter.

Then he called 57, and the halls rang with laughter.

After several minutes, one prisoner was still rolling on the floor laughing.

More minutes - still laughing.

Rocky rapped on the cell wall.

"Yeah, waddaya want?" asked the other inmate.

"I don't understand it," asked Rocky, "Why is Bill still laughing?" "Well," said the gruff inmate, "He never heard that one before!"

Prison Job

Several years ago, Andy was sentenced to prison.

During his stay, he got along well with the guards and all his fellow inmates.

The warden saw that deep down, Andy was a good person and made arrangements for Andy to learn a trade while doing his time.

After three years, Andy was recognized as one of the best carpenters in the local area.

Often he would be given a weekend pass to do odd jobs for the citizens of the community....

and he always reported back to prison before Sunday night was over.

Next Page

Prison Job ...continued

The warden was thinking of remodeling
his kitchen and in fact had done much of
the work himself.
But he lacked the skills to build a set of
kitchen cupboards and a large counter
top which he had promised his wife.
So he called Andy into his office and
asked him to complete the job for him.
But, alas, Andy refused.
He told the warden, "Gosh, I'd really like
to help you but counter fitting is what
got me into prison in the first place".

Too Honest Wife

John & Jessica were on their way home from the bar one night and John got pulled over by the police. The officer told John that he was stopped because his tail light was burned out.

John said, "I'm very sorry officer, I didn't realize it was out, I'll get it fixed right away." Just then Jessica said, "I knew this would happen when I told you two days ago to get that light fixed." So the officer asked for John's license and after looking at it said, "Sir your license has expired." And again John apologized and mentioned that he didn't realize that it had expired and would take care of it first thing in the morning.

Jessica said, "I told you a week ago that the state sent you a letter telling you that your license had expired." Well by this time, John is a bit upset with his wife contradicting him in front of the officer, and he said in a rather loud voice, "Jessica, will you shut up!" The officer then leaned over toward Jessica and asked.

"Does your husband always talk to you like that?" Jessica replied, "only when he's drunk."

Drinking Friends

A man stumbles up to the only other patron in a bar and asks if he could buy him a drink.

"Why, of course," comes the reply.

The first man then asks, "Where are you from?" "I'm from Ireland," replies the second man.

The first man responds by saying, "You don't say. I'm from Ireland too. Let's have another round to Ireland." "Of course," replies the second man.

Curious, the first man then asks, "Where in Ireland are you from?" "Dublin," comes the reply.

"I can't believe it," says the first man, "I'm from Dublin too.

Let's have another drink to Dublin." "Of course," replies the second man.

Curiosity again strikes and the first man asks, "What school did you go to?" "St Mary's,' replies the second man, 'I graduated in 1962." "This is unbelievable," the first man says.

"I went to St Mary's and I graduated in 1962 too."

About that time, one of the regulars comes in and sits down at the bar.

"What's been going on?" he asks the barman.

"Nothing much," replies the barman.

"'The O'Malley twins are drunk again."

Overserved

A guy stumbles through the front door of a bar, ambles up to the bartender and orders a beer. The bartender looks at the drunk man and says,"I'm sorry sir, but I can't serve you...you've already had too much to drink." The guy swears and walks out of the bar.

Five minutes later the guy comes flying through the side door of the bar, and yells for a beer. Again the bartender says,"I'm sorry, sir...but I can't serve you...you've already had too much to drink!" Ten minutes later, the same guy comes through the back door of the bar, storms up to the bartender, and demands a beer.

Again, the bartender says to the man..."I'm really sorry, sir, but you've had too much to drink...you're going to have to leave!" The guy looks quizzically at the bartender and says finally, "My God, man...
How many bars do you work at?!!!"

Speak to the Manager

A rather attractive woman goes up to the bar in a quiet rural pub.

She gestures alluringly to the bartender who comes over immediately.

When he arrives, she seductively signals that he should bring his face close to hers.

When he does so, she begins to gently caress his beard which is full and bushy.

"Are you the manager?" she asked, softly stroking his face with both hands.

"Actually, no," he replied.

"Can you get him for me?

I need to speak to him," she said, running her hands up beyond his beard and into his hair.

"I'm afraid I can't," breathes the bartender, clearly in trouble.

"Is there anything I can do?" "Yes there is.

I need you to give him a message," she continues huskily, popping a couple of fingers into his mouth and allowing him to suck them gently.

"Tell him that there is no toilet paper in the ladies room."

What Goes Around...

Three men died in a car accident and met Jesus himself at the Pearly Gates.

The Lord spoke unto them saying, "I will ask you each a simple question. If you tell the truth I will allow you into heaven, but if you lie...Hell is waiting for you."

To the first man the Lord asked, "How many times did you cheat on your wife?" The first man replied, "Lord, I was a good husband. I never cheated on my wife." The Lord replied, "Very good! Not only will I allow you in, but for being faithful to your wife I will give you a huge mansion and a limo for your transportation."

To the second man the Lord asked, "How many times did you cheat on your wife?" The second man replied, "Lord, I cheated on my wife twice." The Lord replied, "I will allow you to come in, but for your unfaithfulness, you will get a four- bedroom house and a BMW."

Next Page ▷

What Goes Around ...continued

To the third man the Lord asked, "So, how many times did you cheat on your wife?" The third man replied, "Lord, I cheated on my wife about 8 times." The Lord replied, "I will allow you to come in, but for your unfaithfulness, you will get a one-room apartment, and a Yugo for your transportation.

A couple hours later the second and third men saw the first man crying his eyes out. "Why are you crying?" the two men asked. "You got the mansion and limo!" The first man replied, "I'm crying because I saw my wife a little while ago, and she was riding a skateboard!"

Heavenly Rewards

A priest and a taxi driver both died and went to heaven. St. Peter was at the Pearly gates waiting for them.

"Come with me", said St. Peter to the taxi driver.

The taxi driver did as he was told and followed St. Peter to a mansion.

It had anything you could imagine from a bowling alley to an Olympic size pool.

"Wow, thank you", said the taxi driver.

Next, St. Peter led the priest to a rugged old shack with a bunk bed and a little old television set.

"Wait, I think you are a little mixed up", said the priest.

"Shouldn't I be the one who gets the mansion? After all I was a priest, went to church every day, and preached God's word." "Yes, that's true. But during your sermons people slept. When the taxi driver drove, everyone prayed."

Old Fred

Old Fred had been a faithful Christian and was in the hospital, near death. The family called their pastor to stand with them. As the pastor stood next to the bed, Old Fred's condition appeared to deteriorate and he motioned frantically for something to write on. The pastor lovingly handed him a pen and a piece of paper, and Old Fred used his last bit of energy to scribble a note, then he died. The pastor thought it best not to look at the note at that time, so he placed it in his jacket pocket. At the funeral, as he was finishing the message, he realized that he was wearing the same jacket that he was wearing when Old Fred died.

He said, "You know, Old Fred handed me a note just before he died. I haven't looked at it, but knowing Fred, I'm sure there's a word of inspiration there for us all."

He opened the note, and read, "Asshole, you're standing on my oxygen tube!"

Honesty Rewarded

No one believes seniors . . . Everyone thinks they are senile.

An elderly couple was celebrating their sixtieth anniversary. The couple had married as childhood sweethearts and had moved back to their old neighborhood after they retired. Holding hands, they walked back to their old school. It was not locked, so they entered, and found the old desk they'd shared, where Jerry had carved I love you, Sally.

On their way back home, a bag of money fell out of an armored car, practically landing at their feet. Sally quickly picked it up and, not sure what to do with it, they took it home. There, she counted the money - fifty thousand dollars!

Jerry said, "We've got to give it back."

Sally said, "Finders keepers. She put the money back in the bag and hid it in their attic."

Next Page >

Honesty Rewarded ...continued

The next day, two police officers were canvassing the neighborhood looking for the money, and knocked on their door. "Pardon me, did either of you find a bag that fell out of an armored car yesterday?" he said.

Sally said, "No."

Jerry said, "She's lying. She hid it up in the attic."

Sally said, "Don't believe him, he's getting senile."

The agents turned to Jerry and began to question him.

One said: "Tell us the story from the beginning."

Jerry said, "Well, when Sally and I were walking home from school yesterday ....."

The first police officer turned to his partner and said, "We're outta here!"

Plane Crash

An airplane was about to crash. There were 4 passengers on board but only 3 parachutes. The 1st passenger said, "I am Stephen King, the best selling author of my time... My millions of fans need me, and I can't afford to die." So he took the 1st pack and left the plane. The 2nd passenger, "I am the Worlds smartest man. The World needs me. I can't die." He took the 2nd pack and jumped out of the plane. The 3rd passenger, the Pope, said to the 4th passenger, a 10 year old schoolboy, "My son, I am old and don't have many years left, you have more years ahead so I will sacrifice my life and let you have the last parachute." The little boy said , "That's okay , Your Holiness, there's a parachute left for you. The Worlds smartest man just took my backpack."

Zen master in New York

The Zen Master is visiting New York City from Tibet. He goes up to a hot dog vendor and says, "Make me one with everything." The hot dog vendor fixes a hot dog and hands it to the Zen Master, who pays with a $20 bill. The vendor puts the bill in the cash box and closes it. "Where's my change?" asks the Zen Master. The vendor responds, "Change must come from within."

Little Johnny Strikes Again

A teacher asked her students to use the word "fascinate" in a sentence.

Mary said, "My family went to the New York City Zoo, and we saw all the animals. It was fascinating."

The teacher said, "That was good Mary, but I wanted you to use the word fascinate."

Sally raised her hand and said, My family went to the Philadelphia Zoo and saw the animals. I was fascinated."

The teacher said, "Good Sally but I want you to use the word fascinate."

Little Johnny raised his hand.

The teacher was hesitant because Johnny was notorious for his bad language. She finally decided there was no way he could damage the word fascinate, so she called on him.

Johnny said loudly, "My sister has a sweater with 10 buttons."

The teacher said, "That was good Johnny. However you did not use the word fascinate in your sentence.

Johnny continued, "But her boobs are so big, she can only fasten eight!"

What's In A Name

John decided to go skiing with his buddy, Keith. So they loaded up John's minivan and headed north.

After driving for a few hours, they got caught in a terrible blizzard. So they pulled into a nearby farm and asked the attractive lady who answered the door if they could spend the night.

"I realize it's terrible weather out there and I have this huge house all to myself, but I'm recently widowed," she explained. "I'm afraid the neighbors will talk if I let you stay in my house."

'Don't worry," John said. "We'll be happy to sleep in the barn. And if the weather breaks, we'll be gone at first light." The lady agreed, and the two men found their way to the barn and settled in for the night.

Come morning, the weather had cleared, and they got on their way.

They enjoyed a great weekend of skiing.

But about nine months later, John got an unexpected letter from an attorney.

Next Page >

What's In A Name ...continued

It took him a few minutes to figure it out, but he finally determined it was from the attorney of the attractive widow he had met on the ski weekend.

He dropped in on his friend Keith and asked, "Keith, do you remember that good-looking widow from the farm we stayed at on our ski holiday up north about 9 months ago?"

"Yes, I do.", said Keith.

"Did you happen to get up in the middle of the night, go up to the house and pay her a visit?"

"Well, um, yes!" Keith said, a little embarrassed about being found out, "I have to admit that I did."

"And did you happen to give her my name instead of telling her your name?"

Keith's face turned beet red and he said, "Yeah, look, I'm sorry, buddy. I'm afraid I did." "Why do you ask?"

"She just died and left me everything."

The Mistress

A husband and wife were having dinner at a very fine restaurant when this absolutely stunning young woman comes over to their table, gives the husband a big kiss, says she'll see him later and walks away. His wife glares at him and says, "Who the hell was that?" "Oh," replies the husband, "she's my mistress." "Well, that's the last straw," says the wife. "I've had enough, I want a divorce." "I can understand that," replies her husband, "but remember, if we get a divorce it will mean no more shopping trips to Paris, no more wintering in Barbados, no more summers in Tuscany, no more Infinities and Lexus's in the garage and no more yacht club. But the decision is yours." Just then, a mutual friend enters the restaurant with a gorgeous babe on his arm. "Who's that woman with Jim? " asks the wife. "That's his mistress," says her husband. "Ours is prettier," she replies.

State of the Art

A rather confident man walks into a bar and takes a seat next to a very attractive woman. He gives her a quick glance, then casually looks at his watch for a moment. The woman notices this and asks, "Is your date running late?" "No," he replies, "I just bought this state-of-the-art watch and I was just testing it." The intrigued woman says, "A state-of-the-art watch? What's so special about it?" "It uses alpha waves to telepathically talk to me," he explains. "What's it telling you now?" she asked. "Well, it says you're not wearing any panties." he said. The woman giggles and replies, "Well it must be broken then because I am wearing panties!" The man explains, "Damn thing must be an hour fast."

Letter to the Lord

A little boy wanted $100 badly and prayed for two weeks but nothing happened.

Then he decided to write a letter to the Lord requesting the $100.

When the postal authorities received the letter addressed to the Lord, USA, they decided to send it to President Trump.

The President was so impressed, touched, and amused that he instructed his secretary to send the little boy a $5.00 bill, as this would appear to be a lot of money to a little boy.

The little boy was delighted with the $5.00, and sat down to write a thank-you note to the Lord.

It said: Dear Lord, Thank you very much for sending me the money.

However, I noticed that for some reason you had to send it through Washington, DC and as usual, those jerks deducted $95.

The Ugly Baby

A woman got on a bus holding a baby. The bus driver said: "That's the ugliest baby I've ever seen." In a huff, the woman slammed her fare into the fare box and took an aisle seat near the rear of the bus. The man seated next to her sensed that she was agitated and asked her what was wrong. "The bus driver insulted me," she fumed. The man sympathized and said: "Why, he's a public servant and shouldn't say things to insult passengers." "You're right," she said. "I think I'll go back up there and give him a piece of my mind." "That's a good idea," the man said. "Here, let me hold your monkey."

Talking Clock

While proudly showing off his new apartment to friends, a college student led the way into the den. "What is the big brass gong and hammer for?" one of his friends asked. "That is the talking clock," the man replied. "How's it work?" the friend asked. "Watch," the student said then proceeded to give the gong an ear shattering pound with the hammer. Suddenly someone screamed from the other side of the wall, "KNOCK IT OFF, YOU JERK! It's two AM!"

The Brothel

Two elderly gents decided they were close to their last days and decided to have a last night on the town. After a few drinks, they ended up at the local brothel.

The madam takes one look at the two geezers and whispered to her manager, "Go up to the first two bedrooms and put an inflatable doll in each bed. These two are so old and drunk , I'm not wasting two of my girls on them. They won't know the difference."

The manager does as he is told and the two men go up stairs and take care of their business.

As they are walking home the first man says "You know, I think my girl was dead!"

"Dead?" Says his friend "Why do you say that?"

"Well she never moved or made a sound all the time I was loving her."

His friend says, "Could be worse, I think mine was a witch."

"A Witch? ...Why the hell would you say that?"

"Well, I was making love to her, kissing her on the neck, and I gave her a little bite, then she farted and flew out the window, and took my teeth with her!"

The Haircut

A teenaged boy had just passed his driving test and inquired of his father as to when they could discuss the use of the car.

His father said he'd make a deal with his son, "You bring your grades up from a C to a B average, study your Bible a little and get your haircut. Then we'll talk about the car."

The boy thought about that for a moment, decided he'd settle for the offer and they agreed on it.

After about six weeks his father said, "Son, you've brought your grades up and I have observed that you have been studying your Bible, but I'm disappointed you haven't had your hair cut."

The boy said, "You know, Dad, I've been thinking about that, and I've noticed in my studies of the Bible that Samon had long hair, John Baptist had long hair, Moses had long hair, and there's even strong evidence that Jesus had long hair."

Dad's reply ..."Did you also notice that they all walked everywhere they went?"

The LOVE Dress

A woman stopped by, unannounced, at her son's house. She knocked on the door and then immediately walked in. She was shocked to see her daughter-in-law lying on the couch, totally naked. Soft music was playing, and the aroma of perfume filled the room.

"What are you doing?!" she asked.

"I'm waiting for Mike to come home from work," the daughter-in-law answered.

"But you're naked!" the mother-in-law exclaimed.

"This is my love dress," the daughter-in-law explained.

"Love dress? But you're naked!"

"Mike loves me and wants me to wear this dress," she explained. "It excites him to no end. Every time he sees me in this dress, he instantly becomes romantic and ravages me for hours on end. He can't get enough of me."
The mother-in-law left.

When she got home, she undressed, showered, put on her best perfume, dimmed the lights, put on a romantic CD, and lay on the couch, waiting for her husband to arrive.

Finally, her husband came home. He walked in and saw her lying there so provocatively.

"What are you doing?" he asked.

"This is my love dress." she whispered sensually.

"Needs ironing," he said. "What's for dinner?"

He never heard the gunshot.

Kids Can Be So Honest

Last night my kids and I were sitting in
the living room, and I said to them.

"I never want to live in a vegetative state,
dependent on some machine and fluids
from a bottle, if that ever happened, just
pull the plug."

They got up , unplugged the computer
and threw out my wine!

The little bastards.

Kids View On Childbirth

Due to a power outage, only one paramedic responded to the call.

The house was very dark so the paramedic asked Kathleen, a 3-yr old girl to hold a flashlight high over Heidi, her pregnant mommy, so he could see while he helped deliver the baby.

Very diligently Kathleen did as she was asked. Heidi pushed and pushed and after a little while, Connor was born.

The paramedic lifted him by his little feet and spanked him on his bottom. Connor began to cry.

The paramedic then thanked Kathleen for her help and asked the wide- eyed little girl what she thought about what she had just witnessed.

Kathleen quickly responded, "He shouldn't have crawled in there in the first place.... smack his butt again!'

Senior Password Update

Please enter your new password.

cabbage

 Sorry, the password must be more than 8 characters.

 boiled cabbage

 Sorry, the password must contain 1 numerical character.

 1 boiled cabbage

 Sorry, the password cannot have blank spaces

50damnboiledcabbages

 Sorry, the password must contain at least one upper case character

 50DAMNEDboiledcabbages

 Sorry the password cannot use more than one upper case character consecutively.

50DamnBoiledCabbagesShovedUpYourAssIfYouDon'tGiveMeAccessNow!

 Sorry, the password cannot contain punctuation.

ReallyPissedOff50DamnBoiledCabbagesShovedUpYourAssIfYouDontGiveMeAccessNow

 Sorry, that password is already in use

Blonde Wish

A blonde, a brunette and a redhead are stuck on an island. One day, the three of them are walking along the beach and discover a magic lamp. They rub and rub, and sure enough, out pops a genie. The genie says, "Since I can only grant three wishes, you may each have one." The brunette says, "I've been stuck here for years. I miss my family, my husband, and my life. I just want to go home." POOF! The brunette gets her wish and she is returned to her family. Then, the red head says, "I've been stuck here for years as well. I miss my family, my husband, and my life. I wish I could go home too." POOF! The redhead gets her wish and she is returned to her family. The blonde starts crying uncontrollably. The genie asks, "My dear, what's the matter?" The blonde whimpers, "I wish my friends were still here."

The Scientific Bra

Dr. Calvin Rickson, a scientist from Texas A&M University has invented a bra that keeps a woman's breasts from jiggling, bouncing up and down, and prevents the nipples from pushing through the fabric when cold weather sets in.

At a news conference, after announcing his invention, a large group of men took Dr. Rickson outside and beat the tar out of him.

Snoring Coach

The high school coaches in Miami, Florida went on a coaches' retreat. To save money they had to room together. No one wanted to room with Coach Daryl because he snored so bad.

They decide it's not fair to make one of them stay with him the whole time, so they vote to take turns.

The first coach sleeps with Daryl and comes to breakfast next morning with his hair a mess, eyes all bloodshot. They say, "Man, what happened to you?"

He said, "Man, that Daryl snored so loud, I watched him all night."

The next night it was a different coach's turn In the morning, same thing — hair all standing up, eyes all bloodshot. They say, "Man, what happened to you? You look awful!" He said, "Man, that Daryl shakes the roof. I watched him all night."

The third night was Frank's turn. Frank was a big burly ex-football player-looking type of man's man.

Next morning, he comes to breakfast bright eyed and bushy tailed "Good morning."

They can't believe it! They say, "Man, what happened?"

He said, "Well, we got ready for bed. I went and tucked Daryl into bed and kissed him good night. He watched me all night long."

You Can't Fix Stupid

Two guys were messing around with a telephone pole and a tape measure. One guy was at the bottom holding one end of the tape and the other was attempting to scurry up the pole with the other end of the tape. I walked up and asked what they were doing. One of the gentlemen said: "We're trying to find out how tall this thing is". Not trying to be a smart alack I said "Why don't you just lay it down and measure it?" With a look that clearly stated I must be a real dummy , he said, "We know how long it is, we just want to find out how tall it is!"

Taxi Driver

A taxi passenger tapped the driver on the shoulder to ask him a question.

The driver screamed, lost control of the car, nearly hit a bus, went up on the footpath, and stopped centimeters from a shop window.

For a second everything went quiet in the cab, then the driver said, "Look mate, don't ever do that again. You scared the daylights out of me!"

The passenger apologized and said, "I didn't realize that a little tap would scare you so much."

The driver replied, "Sorry, it's not really your fault. Today is my first day as a cab driver - I've been driving a funeral van for the last 25 years".

Potty Pass

Tyler was excited about his first day at school. So excited in fact, that only a few minutes after class started, he realized that he desperately needed to go to the bathroom. So, Tyler raised his hand politely to ask if he could be excused. Of course, the teacher said yes, but asked Tyler to be quick. Five minutes later Tyler returned, looking more desperate and embarrassed. "I can't find it," he admitted. The teacher sat Tyler down and drew him a little diagram to where he should go and asked him if he will be able to find it now. Tyler looked at the diagram, said "yes" and goes on his way. Well, five minutes later he returned to the class room and says to the teacher, "I can't find it." Frustrated, the teacher asked Tommy, a boy who has been at the school for a while, to help him find the bathroom. So, Tommy and Tyler go together and five minutes later they both return r and sit down at their seats. The teacher asks Tommy, "Well, did you find it?" Tommy is quick with his reply, "Oh sure, he just had his boxer shorts on backwards."

Politicians

Five surgeons are discussing who makes the best patients to operate on.

The first surgeon, says, "I like to see accountants on my operating table because when you open them up, everything inside is numbered."

The second, responds, "Yeah, but you should try electricians! Everything inside them is color-coded."

The third surgeon, says, "I really think librarians are the best! Everything inside is in alphabetical order."

The fourth surgeon, chimes in: "You know, I like construction workers. Those guys always understand when you have a few parts left over."

But the fifth surgeon topped them all. "You're all wrong," he said. "Politicians are the easiest to operate on. There's no guts, no heart, no balls, no brains, and no spine . . .. Plus, the head and the butts are interchangeable!"

Bedroom Statue

A woman was in bed with her young lover when she heard her husband opening the front door.

"Hurry, she said, stand in the corner."

She rubbed Baby Oil all over him, and then totally dusted him all over with Talcum Powder.

"Right, don't move until I tell you," she said.

"Just pretend you're a Statue."

"What's this..?" the husband inquired as he entered the room.

"Oh it's a statue." she replied. The Smiths bought one and I liked it so much I got one for us, too."

No more was said, not even when they went to bed.

Around 2am the husband got up, went to the kitchen and returned with a sandwich and a beer.

"Here," he said to the statue, "have this. I stood like that for two f****** days at the Smiths and nobody offered me a damned thing. "

Sunday Morning Sex

Upon hearing that her elderly grandfather had just passed away, Katie went straight to her grandparents house to visit her 95-year-old grandmother and comfort her. When she asked how her grandfather had died, her grandmother replied, "He had a heart attack while we were making love on Sunday morning."

Horrified, Katie told her grandmother that 2 people nearly 100 years old having sex would surely be asking for trouble.

"Oh no, my dear," replied granny. "Many years ago, realizing our advanced age, we figured out the best time to do it was when the church bells would start to ring. It was just the right rhythm. Nice and slow and even & Nothing too strenuous, simply in on the Ding and out on the Dong."

She paused to wipe away a tear, and continued, "He'd still be alive if the ice cream truck hadn't come along."

Engine Trouble

Taxiing down the tarmac, the jetliner abruptly stopped, turned around and returned to the gate. After an hour-long wait, it finally took off. A concerned passenger asked the flight attendant, "What was the problem?" "The pilot was bothered by a noise he heard in the engine," explained the flight attendant, "and it took us a while to find a new pilot."

Police Stop

A driver was pulled over by a police officer for speeding. As the officer was writing the ticket, he noticed several machetes in the car. "What are those for?" he asked suspiciously. "I'm a juggler," the man replied. "I use those in my act." "Well, show me," the officer demanded, still a little unsure. So he got out the machetes and started juggling them, first three, then more, finally seven at one time, overhand, underhand, behind the back, putting on a dazzling show and amazing the officer. Just then another car passed by. The driver did a double take, and said, "That's it Maude. I've got to give up the drink! Just look at the sobriety test they're giving now!!"

The Prescription

A nice, calm and respectable lady went into the pharmacy, walked right up to the pharmacist, looked him straight into his eyes, and said, "I would like to buy some cyanide." The pharmacist asked, "Why in the world do you need cyanide?" The lady replied, "I need it to poison my husband." The pharmacists eyes got big and he exclaimed, "Lord have mercy! I can't give you cyanide to kill your husband! That's against the law! I'll lose my license! They'll throw both of us in jail! All kinds of bad things will happen. Absolutely not! You CANNOT have any cyanide!" The lady reached into her purse and pulled out a picture of her husband in bed with the pharmacist's wife. The pharmacist looked at the picture and replied, "Well now. That's different. You didn't tell me you had a prescription."

The Race

There was a man named Cletus that lived in a small town with only one traffic light. Cletus had saved up his money and bought a mo-ped. One day Cletus was at the light waiting for it to turn green when a shiny new Corvette convertible pulled up next to him. Cletus had never seen anything like this in his life. The Corvette had its top down so Cletus leans over the side of the car and starts checking out the interior. This annoys the driver of the vette so when the light turns green he steps on the gas, laying down rubber as he leaves the intersection. He gets up to 60mph when suddenly Cletus flies by him on his mo-ped. The driver of the vette says to himself "This clown wants to race". Shifting into 4th gear he steps on the gas again. He leaves Cletus in his dust as he gets up to 100mph. Then out of nowhere he sees Cletus coming up fast in his rear view mirror. He can't believe it as Cletus flies by him again on his mo-ped. The driver of the vette shifts into 6th gear and floors it. He passes Cletus and gets up to 150mph! Once again, Cletus passes him like he's standing still. Shocked, the driver of the vette pulls over to the side of the road. He hears gravel flying and brakes squalling as Cletus pulls up next to him. The driver of the vette congratulates Cletus on winning the race and asks him what kind of an engine he has in his mo-ped. Puzzled Cletus replied "Race? I was just trying to get my suspenders off of your side-view mirror."

FIRE!

There was a Texas oil tycoon who was watching his largest oil well going up in flames. He called in the best fire fighting equipment money could buy but there was no way they could get close enough to the intense flames to reach them with their water hose. Finally, out of desperation, he called the local volunteer fire department. They chugged up in their 1946 truck and passed every one of the state of the art rigs and headed toward the center of the fire. They stopped, jumped out, sprayed each other down with water, and then proceeded to put out the fire. When they were finally finished, the millionaire was so impressed with the crew's dedication and bravery, he awarded the chief with a check for $10,000. Later, a reporter asked the chief what he was going to do with the money. The chief replied, "Well, the first thing we're going to do is fix those lousy brakes!!"

Poachers

A game warden stops a poacher walking along the beach and tells him he's going to fine him for taking lobsters without a permit. The poacher tells the warden the two lobsters in his hands are his pets and he was just taking them for a walk. "Nonsense," says the game warden. "It's true, it's not against the law to walk your pets along the beach, is it?" asks the man. "I send them into the surf for a swim and when I whistle they come back to me". "I've got to see this; show me." says the game warden. So the man tosses both lobsters into the ocean and the game warden says, "Okay, now let's hear you whistle for your lobsters to swim back to you." "Lobsters?" asks the poacher, "What lobsters?"

The Memorial

One Saturday morning, the pastor noticed little Johnny was staring up at the large plaque that hung in the foyer of the church. It was covered with names, and small American flags were mounted on either side of it. The seven-year old had been staring at the plaque for some time, so the pastor walked up, stood beside the boy, and said quietly, "Good morning Johnny." "Good morning pastor Ron," replied the young man, still focused on the plaque. "Pastor, what is this?" Johnny asked. "Well, son, it's a memorial to all the young men and women who died in the service." Soberly, they stood together, staring at the large plaque. Little Johnny's voice was barely audible when he asked, "Which one, the Wednesday night or Sunday morning service?"

A Drunks Wisdom

A woman was shopping at her local supermarket where she selected a half-gallon of 2% milk, a carton of eggs, a quart of orange juice, a head of romaine lettuce, a 2 lbs can of coffee, and a 1 lb package of bacon.

As she was unloading her items on the conveyor belt to check-out, a drunk standing behind her watched as she placed the items in front of the cashier. While the cashier was ringing up her purchases the drunk calmly stated, "You must be single."

The woman was a bit startled by this proclamation but she was equally intrigued by the derelict's intuition since she was indeed single.

She looked at her six items on the belt and saw nothing particularly unusual about her selections that could have tipped off her drunken observer as to her marital status.

Curiosity getting the better of her, she said, "Well, you know what, you're absolutely correct. But how on earth did you know that?"

The drunk replied, "Cause you're ugly."

Bird Brain

One day a man strolled in to the paint section of a hardware store and walked up to the assistant. "I'd like a pint of canary colored paint," he says. "Sure" the clerk replies. "Mind if I ask what it's for?" "My parakeet, "the man said. "See, I want to enter him in a canary contest. He sings so beautifully he is sure to win." "Well, you can't do that!" the assistant says. "The chemicals in the paint will surely kill the poor thing!" "No they won't," says the customer. "Listen, buddy, I'll bet you twenty bucks your parakeet dies if you try to paint him." "You're on" said the customer. Two days later the man walks back in the store and very sheepishly lays $20 on the counter. "So the paint killed him?" asked the clerk. "Indirectly," the man said. "He seemed to handle the paint okay, but I think the sanding between coats did him in."

Headhunters

A missionary was going in to the most remote section of Africa. He found a native that would take him upstream to a tribe of headhunters cut off from civilization. In the distance they could hear drums. "What is that drumming?" he asked nervously. The native replied, "Drums okay, but if they stop it would be very bad".

The drums continued for 3 days as they got closer to the headhunters' village. Then without warning the drums suddenly stopped. The forest fell eerily silent. With panic in his voice, the missionary calls out to the guide, "The drums have stopped! What happens now?" The guide crouched down, covered his head with his hands and with despair in his voice, answered, "Tuba solo."

Strike One

A neighbor was watching a little boy playing with a ball and bat in his backyard. "I'm the greatest hitter in the world" the boy exclaimed as he threw the ball into the air. He swung with all his might but missed the ball and fell down himself. "Strike One" he says as he gets up. He throws it up again and swings. Again the ball falls to the ground with a thud. "Strike Two" he yells still undeterred. "I'm the greatest" he says as he swings once again hitting only air as the ball falls to the ground. This time he dances around the backyard as he yells "Strike Three.... I'm the greatest pitcher in the world!"

Cleaned with Coldwater

A man went to visit his 90 year old grandfather in a secluded, rural area of the state. After spending the night, his grandfather prepared breakfast for him consisting of eggs and bacon. He noticed a film-like substance on his plate and he questioned his grandfather....are these plates clean?

His grandfather replied.... those plates are as clean as cold water can get them so go on and finish your meal. That afternoon, while eating the hamburgers his grandfather made for lunch, he noticed tiny specks around the edge of this plate, and a substance that looked like dried egg yolks...so he asked again......are you sure these plates are clean?

Without looking up from his hamburger, the grandfather says.....I told you before, those dishes are as clean as cold water can get them, now don't ask me about it anymore!

Later that afternoon, he was on his way out to get dinner in a nearby town. As he was leaving, Grandfather's dog started to growl and would not let him pass.... Grandfather, your dog won't let me out. Without diverting his attention from the football game he was watching, Grandfather shouted,

"COLDWATER, GET OUT OF THE WAY!!"

Secret To A Long Marriage

A couple was celebrating their golden wedding anniversary. Their domestic tranquility had long been the talk of the town. A local newspaper reporter was inquiring as to the secret of their long and happy marriage. "Well, it dates back to our honeymoon," explained the man. "We visited the Grand Canyon and took a trip down to the bottom on the canyon by pack mule.

We hadn't gone too far when my wife's mule stumbled. My wife quietly said, 'That's once.' We proceeded a little further and the mule stumbled again. Once more my wife quietly said, 'That's twice.' Hadn't gone a half- mile when the mule stumbled the third time. My wife quietly removed a revolver from her pocket and shot the mule dead. I started to yell at her for her treatment of the mule when she looked at me and quietly said 'That's once."

Grandma

A family took their frail, elderly mother to a nursing home and left her, hoping she would be well cared for. The next morning, the nurses bathed her, fed her a tasty breakfast, and set her in a chair at a window overlooking a lovely flower garden. She seemed okay, but after a while she slowly started to tilt sideways in her chair. Two attentive nurses immediately rushed up to catch her and straighten her up. Again she seemed okay, but after a while she slowly started to tilt over to her other side. The nurses rushed back and once more brought her back upright. This went on all morning. Later, the family arrived to see how the old woman was adjusting to her new home.

"So Ma, how is it here? Are they treating you all right?"

"It's pretty nice," she replied. "Except they won't let me pass gas."

City Slickers

A family from the hills of Kentucky was visiting the big city for the first time. They stayed in a high rise hotel with a big brass elevator right off of the lobby. The father and son stared at it in amazement, wondering what it was. After staring at it in awe for a few minutes the boy looked up at his dad, "Pa, what do you reckon that there thing is?" he asked. "I don't rightly know, son." the father replied. Just then an old, frumpy woman with curlers in her hair walks up, steps on the elevator and the doors shut behind her. After about 30 seconds the doors opened again and a beautiful, young blonde wearing a mini-skirt walks out. The father leans over to his son and says, "Boy, go and git your Ma!"

Where Is God?

A Sunday School teacher of preschoolers was concerned that his student might be a little confused about Jesus Christ because of the Christmas season emphasis on His birth. He wanted to make sure they understood that the birth of Jesus occurred for real. He asked his class, "Where is Jesus today?" Steven raised his hand and said, "He's in heaven." Mary was called on and answered, "He's in my heart." Little Johnny, waving his hand furiously, blurted out, "I know, I know! He's in our bathroom!!!" The whole class got very quiet, looked at the teacher, and waited for a response. The teacher was completely at a loss for a few very long seconds. Finally, he gathered his wits and asked Little Johnny how he knew this. Little Johnny said, "Well... every morning, my father gets up, bangs on the bathroom door, and yells, "Good Lord, are you still in there?!"

The Wreck

A lady had just totaled her car in a horrific accident. Miraculously, she managed to pry herself from the wreckage without a scratch and was applying fresh lipstick when the state trooper arrived. "My Goodness!" the trooper gasped. "Your car looks like an accordion that was stomped on by an elephant. Are you OK ma'am?" "Why, yes, officer, I'm just fine" the lady chirped. "Well, how in the world did this happen?" the officer asked as he surveyed the wrecked car. "Officer, it was the strangest thing!" the lady began. "I was driving along this road when I started to doze off. When I woke up this TREE from out of nowhere pops up in front of me. So I swerved to the right, and there was another tree! I swerved to the left and there was ANOTHER tree! I swerved to the right and there was another tree! I swerved to the left and there was...." "Uh, ma'am, 'the officer said, cutting her off, "There isn't a tree on this road for 30 miles. That was your air freshener swinging back and forth on your rear view mirror."

Lawyer Test

You know it's time to get a new lawyer when :

- The prosecutor sees your lawyer in the hall, and they high-five each other.

- During your initial consultation he tries to sell you Amway.

- He tells you that his last good case was a "Pepsi."

- He picks the jury by playing "duck-duck-goose."

- During the trial you catch him playing his Gameboy.

- Just before he says "Your Honor," he makes those little quotation marks in the air with his fingers.

- Whenever his objection is overruled, he tells the judge, "Whatever."

- He giggles every time he hears the word "briefs."

- He keeps citing the legal case of Godzilla v. Mothra.

- He begins closing arguments with, "As Ally McBeal once said..."

Aging Gracefully

- I finally got my head together, now my body is falling apart.
- When did my wild oats turn to prunes and All Bran?
- Funny, I don't remember being absent minded.
- If all is not lost, where is it?
- It was all so different before everything changed.
- Some days you're the dog, some days you're the hydrant.
- Nostalgia isn't what it used to be.
- I wish the buck stopped here. I could use a few.
- The only time the world beats a path to your door is if you're in the bathroom.
- If God wanted me to touch my toes, he would have put them on my knees.
- When you're finally holding all the cards, why does everyone else decide to play cards?
- Health is merely the slowest possible rate at which one can die.
- It's not hard to meet expenses....they're everywhere.
- I started out with nothing...I still have most of it.

Bumpersnickers

- "The gene pool could use a little chlorine."
- "Change is inevitable, except from a vending machine."
- "Time is what keeps everything from happening at once."
- "I love cats...they taste just like chicken"
- "The more people I meet, the more I like my dog."
- "Laugh alone and the world thinks you're an idiot."
- "I get enough exercise just pushing my luck!"
- "Sometimes I wake up grumpy; Other times I let her sleep"
- "I want to die in my sleep like my grandfather.... Not screaming and yelling like the passengers in his car"
- "I didn't fight my way to the top of the food chain to be a vegetarian."
- "Where there's a will, I want to be in it!"
- "If we aren't supposed to eat animals, why are they made of meat?"
- "IRS: We've got what it takes to take what you've got."

You're In A Redneck Church If...

- The finance committee refuses to provide funds for the purchase of a chandelier because none of the members know how to play it.

- People ask, when Jesus fed 5000, whether the two fish were bass or catfish, and what bait was used to catch 'em.

- The pastor says, "I'd like to ask Bubba to help take up the offering," then five guys and two women stand up.

- Opening day of deer season is recognized as an official church holiday.

- A member of the church requests to be buried in his 4-wheel-drive truck because "It ain't never been in a hole it couldn't get out of."

- The choir is known as the "OK Chorale".

- With a congregation of 500 members, there are only seven last names in the church directory.

-High notes on the organ make all the dogs sleeping on the church floor
begin to howl.

-People think "rapture" is what you get when you lift something too heavy.

What is She Doing?

One day a blond went out to check her mail box. There was nothing in it. Her neighbor who was also out there gives her a weird look. An hour later she goes back out to her mailbox and goes back in cause there was nothing in it and her neighbor goes "What the hell is she doing?" An hour later she goes back out side and looks in the mailbox and there is nothing in it. Finally the neighbor gets curious enough to ask her what she is doing. The blonde says, "My stupid computer keeps saying you've got mail."

No Good Deed...

A man is walking down the street one day when he notices a very small boy trying to press a doorbell on a house across the street. However, the boy is very small and the doorbell is too high for him to reach. After watching the boy's efforts for some time, the man moves closer to the boy's position. He steps smartly across the street, walks up behind the little fellow and, placing his hand kindly on the child's shoulder, leans over and gives the doorbell a solid ring. Crouching down to the childs level, the man smiles benevolently and asks, "And now what, my little man?" The boy replies, "Now we run!"

Little Johnny

Little Johnny came home from school with a note from his teacher saying that Johnny was having trouble telling the difference between boys and girls, and would his mother please sit down and have a talk with Johnny about this. So Johnny's mother takes him quietly by the hand upstairs to her bedroom, and closes the door. "First, Johnny, I want you to take off my blouse", she said, so Johnny unbuttons her blouse and takes it off. "O.K., now take off my skirt", and he takes off her skirt. "Now take off my bra", which he does. "And now, Johnny, please take off my panties". Johnny finishes removing these too. His mother then says, "Johnny, please don't wear any of my clothes to school anymore!"

Happy Halloween

It was Halloween and three vampires went into a saloon and bellied up to the bar. "What will you have?" the bartender asked. "I'll have a glass of blood," the first replied. "I'll have a glass of blood, too, please," said the second. "I'll have a glass of plasma," said the third. "OK, let me get this straight," the bartender said. "That will be two bloods and a blood light?"

Bikers and The Truck Driver

A grizzled old man was eating in a truck stop when three Hell's Angels' bikers walked in. The first walked up to the old man, pushed his cigarette into the old man's pie and then took a seat at the counter. The second walked up to the old man, spat into the old man's milk and then he too took a seat at the counter. The third walked up to the old man, turned over the old man's plate, and then he took a seat at the counter. Without a word of protest, the old man quietly left the diner. Shortly thereafter, one of the bikers said to the waitress, "Humph, not much of a man, was he?" The waitress replied, "Not much of a truck driver either, he just backed his big-rig over three motorcycles."

The Day Off

So you want a day off. Let's take a look at what you are asking for. There are 365 days per year available for work. There are 52 weeks per year in which you already have 2 days off per week, leaving 261 days available for work. Since you spend 16 hours each day away from work, you have used up 170 days, leaving only 91 days available. You spend 30 minutes each day on coffee break which counts for 23 days each year, leaving only 68 days available.

With a 1 hour lunch each day, you used up another 46 days, leaving only 22 days available for work. You normally spend 2 days per year on sick leave. This leaves you only 20 days per year available for work. We are off 5 holidays per year, so your available working time is down to 15 days. We generously give 14 days vacation per year which leaves only 1 day available for work and I'll be damned if you are going to take that day off!

What Do You Think?

3 guys go for dinner, each buys a $10 steak. At the end of the meal, they collect $30 between the three of them to cover the cost of the meals and gives it to the waitress. She goes back to the cash register, where the overlooking manager says "Those dinners are discounted, you need to give them $5 back." So the waitress gets the five dollars, and returns to the table. Not knowing how to split $5 between the three of them, she gives 1 dollar to each of the three patrons, and kept two for herself.

Now if you do the math, together they paid $30, got $3 back meaning they only paid $27. The waitress kept $2. This totals $29. Where did the last dollar go?

Made in the USA
Middletown, DE
08 May 2019